Stepping Stones

Sheila Bautista

DEDICATION

I dedicate this to all my readers who are currently hurting, healing, looking to follow God, or for those who simply love to love. May this book help you heal, help you become better, spiritually, internally and externally. I pray that this book may help you reach for a hand with Jesus to get closer to God. I hope my poetry can touch your soul the way I expressed mine by writing this.

Special thanks to my parents, for everything.

CONTENTS

ACKNOWLEDGMENTS

I want to acknowledge the few people who knew about my poetry and always motivated me to never give up on it. For a long time I kept my poetry a secret and the few people who knew about it always motivated me to continue with it. I want to acknowledge my 6th grade writing teacher, she helped me develop my true passion for writing poetry. I also want to acknowledge my freshmen year of college Creative Poetry professor for inspiring me and teaching me skills I hadn't yet known to become a better poet. Lastly, I want to acknowledge you if you are reading this book right now, for I hope I can connect with your soul through my way of expressing art.

1 Types of Love

Madre Mia

My mother has immigrant written across her lips

English more broken than her marriage turned out to
be.

Upon arriving

Land of the free turned out to be

Land of the worry.

She is my heart.

I do this to promise you I will not take you risking your
life for granted mama.

True Love

My mother immigrated to Puerto Rico when she was about 25. She had to leave her 5 month old first born baby girl in Dominican Republic. My mom had to leave everything, her family, husband, friends, job, she had to start over. But she did it because America is known to be the country of success. She was willing to give up her life to find the best future for her newborn daughter and for her two other children which at the time she probably didn't know she was going to have.

The Beginning:

15 years old seems awfully young

Awfully beautiful

Awfully innocent

16 is still young

2 young minds make an old one together

Too young to be committed into something you don't fully understand

I knew what I thought I knew

He knew what he thought he knew too

We both knew nothing

2 of my adolescent years were spent hopelessly

Hopelessly thinking I was in love

I don't regret it

Or him

I was 17 when you left

By the end I was glad.

 You will always be my first attempt at love.

Who's at fault ?

falling into the right one

 is never the right time

         either i'm too in love

               or he is too blind

                  tell him i'm not the one for him

                     but he doesn't want to leave me

                        i don't know why i'm like
this

                          i push the good
ones

                             away from
me,

            maybe it's because i never saw real love.

            stop blaming others for your inability to
love

                        i can not stop.

Love Story

I had a crush on you

From afar, I kept it a secret for so long

By the way you looked at me crushing me even more with your big almond eyes.

I thought you had crushed on me too.

I told you my secret

that you were my crush.

The only thing crushed after, was my heart…

once I realized I had just been dumped

from my fairytale

Alcohol is a man's best friend:

My first love should've been my father

I searched in him what my father lacked in giving me

Protection

Encouragement

A feeling of never ending love

I know my father loves me

He just has a different way of showing it

Sometimes he just needs help from the whiskey in his cup

Few shots down and I am reminded of how much he loves me.

My father is different

Instead of showing me how much he loves me through actions

He shows me by making up from loss time

He hands me green papers who have old presidents on them.

Father, the only old man I want to be holding, is you.

When I was younger my siblings and I would never hug each other. Only on New Years when the clock hit 12 and everyone else would hug. We were scared to be the one to break the non affectionate relationship we had created.

You never know when the last chance to hug someone might be.

Confused love

I think i'm too young for love

Apart of me wants to be with this same person until we grow old together

The other half of me is selfish

You are so sweet to me

So kind and loving

I have no reason to leave you

But that of my selfish ways

This time the love feels real

18 and I feel as though you are the one

How does anyone really know who is the one?

3 billion people on this planet

1 is meant for you.

I want to be with you forever

But forever doesn't want me to be with you.

Every time

Every time I think about you,

I thank God for placing us together

I thank God for placing you in my life at the perfect
time

I didn't even know I needed someone like you in my
life

Until I finally got to have you.

Don't ever want you to leave my side

Don't ever want you to say goodbye.

From the moment you leave,

I miss you

From the moment we are together,

I always want to kiss you.

I could hug you forever

I don't ever want you to let me go.

And when we are at our lowest point,

And we are both ready to give up

We must hug each and hold each other even tighter

Because with each other we are secure

We share a connection that I have never felt before.

You caught my breath

With every sweet spoken word that speaks through you.

Every action you do for me,

I appreciate more than words can ever describe

More than I'll ever be able to describe.

I feel it in me,

You are the one I will marry and have my kids with.

Your encouraging words brighten up my heart and day.

Every goodnight kiss,

Warms my heart like a ray of light

You are my ray of light

I will love you forever.

Timeless

Every moment I spend with you is timeless

I look into your eyes and see time fly by

I see our future together in the blink of an eye

Our future kids holding our hands

And walking by our side

And us two walking down the aisle

me as your bride

I do not want to rush time

And sometimes I wish I could press rewind

Rewind to when I met you to relive that moment

all over again.

Sometimes I wish I can pause time

To pause the clock during moments in which I lay with you

For every second of every minute of every hour of every day

I always want to be next to you.

"Above all, love each other deeply, because love covers over a multitude of sins."

-John 15:12:

2 Awareness

Good morning

She sighs without knowing what her day will consist of

As if everyday was programed to be the same

As if there isn't 1440 minutes in one day

She seems to not know that every minute counts

Whether you are 14 or 40 you do have a say.

She forgets that she is not the only one living

That there are struggles bigger than hers

There's a whole other world she has no clue about

Yet she always seems to be stuck in her own.

Emergency

Firefighters speed at 97 miles per hour down my street

Rush of sadness remains

The rapidity of the wind is left behind the truck, and
out into the openness of my street

For everyone to watch and see

Someone is either,

dying,

scared,

sick,

or already dead.

Police sirens go off at the speed of light

All cars turn their wheels and make a clear open drive
way for the police cars to speed off into and disappear

Someone is either,

in danger,

worried,

or victimized

Atoms fall from their eyes, down their cheek as a clear
liquid substance

They are either,

In pain,

In shock,

Or happy.

The Clock is Always Ticking

The present is now

and the past

 is every second before that,

then,

> when are we ever living in the present ?

> If each second that passes is the past...
When do we get to enjoy the present ?

> Being able to stay present, is a present.

> Be mindful…

> Time doesn't stop.

Elevator of Life

I step foot into the elevator door

In a building that has endless amount of floors

I look at all the numbers and press the 20th floor

I'm only at the second and the elevator stops

The door opens

A person comes in delaying my ride

They press the floor number 15.

The 4th floor arrives, and the elevator stops and opens
up again

Allowing for 2 more people to enter

But we all have different destinations

People come in and go out

Some chat with me as we wait for each others stops

Some don't talk to me at all

Some reach the 20th floor with me

While some I watch leave

In the end we all reach our destination.

Bully

i wake up bruised from the day before

My bully left me swollen eyed

Giving me a blurred vision

i try to tell myself i'm okay and i can make it through the day

But then she gets me

She finds me when i am most weakened

She finds me when i am vulnerable

And desperate

Intimated by her i turn around and forget

About where i was heading

She's always making me change my mind

At the time when i need the most encouragement.

i get put down by her the most

i wish someone could beat her up for me

But cognitive distortions is something only I can beat

Stay Woke

From the first day we start our first year in education, to our very last day in high school, we have always been told that college is the most important aspect in life in order to have a "successful career". Although at the age of five, and even eleven, they don't throw at you the expenses colleges brings, the loans you'll most likely have to take out, and the interests for taking loans out that you'll have to pay once you graduate. There was a time period in my life when I learned most colleges are more than what my mom makes annually... I got scared

I do not want to get stuck in the intergenerational transmission of economic status that families living in poverty face in the U.S.

I will not be another statistic.

Be Thankful

When I was younger and wanted the new pair of Heelys shoes that commercials kept advertising

the cool sneakers with wheels on the back of their shoes.

The cool kids owned a pair.

I remember asking my mom for them.

In response she told me that when she was younger she had to be lucky enough to even find two of the same shoes to go to school.

Some days she would have to go with a broken shoe

and later ask her mom to sew it back on for the third time.

As an 8 year old, I was just mad she didn't want to buy me the damn shoes.

As I got older, I realized there is so much more behind that story.

Open Your Eyes

The first step to everything is becoming aware of the problem,

without being aware,

you'll never notice anything wrong.

Notice It

The root of jealousy comes from people lacking the ability to realize that their time will come.

Sometimes it's uncontrollable

And you don't even realize that you're jealous.

But as soon as you do…stop your self

And think about why?

Stop yourself and analyze

That their will come a time

Where you will want others to be happy for you,

Not jealous.

Stop letting your own self doubts get in the way of being happy for someone else

We. Can. All. Win.

Just in different ways

In the end, we're not all meant to be the same person in life anyways.

We all shine on different days.

"Thieves are jealous of each others loot,

but the godly are well rooted and bear their own fruit."

-Proverbs 12:12

3 We All Bleed Red

ALL COLORS BLEED RED

When the white man opens his mouth there are two tongues inside

When the black man opens his mouth it is empty

Why does it always have to be about race?

Because society has made it that way

Put an asterisk next to a dark girls face, call her pretty… *for a black girl

When people tell immigrants to go back home, if only they meant to the apartment down the street

But I know back home is a foreign land they wish to exile colored people in

Because it is easier to destroy something you do not understand, than it is to embrace it.

DEAR BLACK GIRLS

DON'T let the colorist of this society make you believe this preconceived notion that your pussy is anything less than valuable.

BLACK pussy is BEAUTIFUL

It is NOT ugly

Nor stinky

Nor dirty

And it is DEFINITELY not trash simply because it is black

It is GOLD.

People are ridiculous to believe your hygiene is defined by the color of your vagina.

Imbeciles, we've had enough.

Sincerely, Sheila after hearing someone say "ew, it looks like a black girls pussy"

p.s. ALL vaginas are pink on the inside.

Racism

A sin so wrong it literally penetrates my soul and cuts through it

Like a sad soul ready to end the life that was given to them

Rest in peace to my ancestors, I did not know them

We are connected by our history

We have fought for the same rights

Based upon the pigmentation of our skin

we have been boxed away and cast down by stereotypes

Under this skin we are all 99.9 percent the same...

This skin is nothing but tissue

But until this is learned, we can not begin

All of our blood is the same,
That runs deep within our veins

With guns they came, with whips and chains
Chains to capture the Dark Continent...

Just because my skin is this way doesn't mean I was intended to be a slave

Modern Slaves

Why is the course of your entire life predicated on the color of your skin?

Why does the amount of melanin in your skin determine so much?

African - Americans were stolen,

traded off and lost among oceans

"free" but their minds still in the chains

dying one by one being killed off by one stereotype after another

And the justice system, is its partner in crime

But look deeper than the color of my skin,

look deep down within.

And problems will begin to fade

when we all can relate

to leave any other division behind

You ask why does it always have to be about race?...

Because society has made it that way.

Aryan Race

Will we become the "Brave New World"?

Not intimidated by all of this

But instead consuming into the production of inequality in every hair perm straightener and bleach cream that is bought?

But don't blame the consumer for wanting this.

Because why are such things even invented?

I live in a society where it's legal to create designer babies

I live in a society where it's acceptable to sterilize eggs in test tubes

I live in a society where human embryos are experimented with and genetically altered

In order to produce a "model child"?

White skin, blue eyes, blonde hair...

Who wants a dark skin, kinky hair, baby?...

Because the darker you are, the more socially unfit you are right?

The more of a burden you are to society right?

The more socially inadequate you are right?...

As dark skinned individuals we are taught:

Have a thinner nose

Have smaller lips

Go straight to jail

Your hair is loud just like you

Keep it tamed and hushed down

Your presence makes me feel unsafe

But Lighter skins... be proud, you're ambiguity is a blessing…

Being undocumented in the U.S is like holding a microphone, but being forbidden from speaking.

Equity

Race is a social invention

Race is a myth

Aimed to place people in a hierarchy

One in which dark people are inhibited from rising up

One in which darker people have a harder time in climbing the stairs of success

Because how can you compare someone who has had all the steps given to them,

to someone who has to build the steps on their own.

It is not about equality,

It is about equity.

<u>Pt. 2</u>

Darker skin has always been something that has been stigmatized and looked down upon.

For this reason,

How was I not to believe that my dark skin was a burden?

Stripped away from our rights of even being considered a human

For centuries.

Questions

How many innocent black lives does it take to stop police brutality ?

How many times does a white police man get to hold power and do Un just before a change is made ?

How many innocent black lives have to get incarcerated before there are none left to able to get employed ?

How many massive shootings done by a white person does it have to take until they ban guns?

Will things ever be the same for us ?

2 words,

Systematic, Racism .

"Anyone who claims to be in the light but hates a brother or sister is still in the darkness."

1 John 2:10

4 Self Realization

Fake Friends

Isolated from the rest I feel I work best

Better than when I sit in a room full of wandering thoughts

Thoughts I have no access to

I hate not having access.

I wish I knew what others thought about me

Then I would know who I could work next to and who I couldn't.

Before It's Too Late

You try to find in others what you never saw in yourself

You believe there is someone above controlling me and you

What you believe you tend to see

You look for him when lost

You get lost within your own ideas

You live without stability

Not knowing what your tomorrow will look like is okay

But not knowing what you want it to look like is frightening

How lost can you be in a world full of directions

How clueless can you be in a world full of answers

You go out there and search for them

If you don't create your own world

The world around you will start creating you instead.

Reflection

I look into the mirror to see myself,

Or is it really me?

More of a reflection of what I want to be,

Never sure about whats in front of me

I try to reassure myself that I know who I am.

But no one knows, that i don't know, who i truly am.

Pop

I am human form of a soda bottle.

    When you shake me and I open up, I explode.

    Unless I've held it in for too long, then I am flat.

Insecurities

I look down at my big thighs

smushed against my now warm toilet seat

From me sitting on it for so long

Sighing at my reality

Picking up the vogue magazine across from me

A tear slaps on my skin, my drum stick

My thighs begin to numb

On the toilet for so long.

My nails engrave white lines scratching my now ashy skin

Creating where I would tell the surgeon to cut off

I want a gap I would say

Not like the one in between my two front teeth

But the one that would let my skin breathe when I walked.

Goal Digger

I can feel it when I think about my future

All that I am

And all that I can be

I get an adrenaline rush just thinking about it

Always thinking about how I can constantly do more,

be more,

 in everything that I to do.

<u>Art</u>

I am an artist

Without using paint.

You see, my form of art involves my body and mind

Without using paint brushes on a canvas

I am both a dancer and a writer

I touch souls differently.

My Addiction

I have an addiction

My addiction allows me to be high

So high.

High up into the sky

My addiction allows me to be in a new space

New environment

New cultural

My addiction allows me to see things I've never seen or experienced before

Meet new people and see things differently

My addiction allows me to explore

I am addicted to traveling.

"Only God gives inward peace, and I depend on Him. God alone is the mighty rock that keeps me safe, and he is the fortress where I feel secure."

- Psalm 62:5-12

5 The Power Faith

Are you Adam or Eve?

We are all in the same garden as Adam and Eve.

Just different temptations,

different sins to be deceived from.

A different form of a snake

disguised as humans.

BFFL

My best friend can listen to me talk for days

Yet never shut me up.

My best friend is the only person I can trust my whole entire life with

My best friend can listen to me vent without any judgment

I can talk to my best friend at 4am or 7pm and they'll always listen

My best friend speaks to me at the times where I need to be spoken to the most

And they always know whats best for me before I even know whats best for my self

My best friend arrives when I least expect it

They never let me feel alone

My best friends name is Jesus Christ, he helps me walk closer

To God

HIM

Who can answer you without saying not one word,

Who can make a miracle out of the midst of adversity

Who can love you even if you hate him

Who can leave you clueless but answer you at the same
time

You're frustrated but he's calm,

You're sad but he's cautious

Through him you are different

You walk different

Act through kindness

Smile at your glory

Ease at your mistakes.

He holds the door open for you while everyone slams it
shut,

He will never neglect you.

Daughter of a King

What you need to understand is you can have everything in the world. A bank account full of money, the newest dream car you've always wanted, family, marriage, and a great job. But until you meet him, encounter him, live with him, you will never be fully happy. Church is one way to help you find Jesus Christ, because only through him will you get closer to God. Jesus himself said this in John: 14:6, " I am the way and the truth and the life. No one comes to the father except through me." Pray, pray and pray. With church or without, praying to him, speaking to him, is one step closer to building an eternal internal life of good grace. God wants to hear you speak to Him.

With believing comes faith. You can't just believe in God and have no faith in Him. You must have faith that what ever happens in life, you pray on it, He hears you, and He decides your future not you. You have no control over what God has planned for you. He plans your destiny and that's why you must not worry. During the good and during the bad, trust in Him, believe in Him, but most importantly, have faith that what is meant for you will be for you because God has a plan solely for you.

Which religion should I follow?

I believe that there is no correct or "right religion". In my eyes, there is no false religion to follow. At the end of the day, what ever you believe in your heart and mind you will create. I know that my God is real, he serves and he stands with me every where and every step I go. The Bible says that if you believe with your heart, and confess with your mouth that God raised his son from the dead, you will be saved. (Romans 10:9).

Remember that it is not about the *religion* you "follow", but about the *relationship* you follow, with God.

How do I start?

You need to feed your faith. Don't just pray, and ask, ask, ask, but give thanks to God, constantly, for everything you have and everything he has done for you in your life. Read your bible and really analyze what the word of God is trying to say to you. That is God himself teaching you a lesson through his words, the closest form of response from Him will be found in the Bible, without a middle man. Be careful and wary of false prophets, as the Bible says, "Do not believe every spirit, but test the spirits to see whether they are from God, for many false prophets have gone out into the world," - Matthew 7:15. Protecting your self from false prophets in the religious world is crucial. That is why you listen, but pray to God that what you are receiving is coming solely and only from Him.

Listen to music that will feed your soul. Wake up first thing in the morning and blast worship music, don't only listen to the lyrics but really dig deep into the lyrics, sing the lyrics and feel the lyrics. When you're in your car ride to work listen to worship music, or listen to a sermon to get you started for the day. When you're scrolling through instagram, find pastors who post the word of God, and prayers and positive spiritual messages on a daily basis so you're constantly feeding your mind with God even when you're on social media too. When you are sad and going through something, do not play sad music of modern culture that will only get you even more saddened. But listen to words of the Holy Spirit, ask Jesus to help you over come those dark times and listen to uplifting worship music that will remind you God can help you get through anything.

Walk That Talk

We are all born sinners, we all sin, even the most holy, sin, we constantly sin through our thoughts and actions. We must ask Jesus Christ to forgive us constantly, not only to forgive us for our sins but to remove us from sinful nature, to guide us to a heart filled with love like our Jesus Christ, ask Him to teach you to have a heart, mind, and soul like His.

We must ask our Lord to clean our hearts and minds, and show him how badly we want to be a kind, spirited, soul. Only then will we begin to talk like Jesus, walk like Jesus, and act like Jesus in the most purest and genuine way. We must show others what having Jesus in our life is like by the way you treat them.

This will allow for Jesus to clean our hearts on a daily basis, and like this we will get closer to our King.

" Repent, then, and turn to God, so that your sins may be wiped out, that times of refreshing may come from the Lord."

Acts 3:19

ABOUT THE AUTHOR

I grew up in Catholic family, a couple religious aunts, one that is a Nun, and some aunts or uncles who haven't stepped foot in a church in over 20 years. My household had an on and off relationship with church growing up. But an everyday relationship with God. Easter was always a must for church attendance. We would have a couple months where we would go every Sunday and some months we'd fall off and not go for a year or 2, besides Easter. But regardless of church attendance, my mother taught me to pray every single night for as long as I can remember speaking. She taught me how to give thanks every single morning for everything that I have because of God. My mother never let a day go by without reminding me to pray each night. My heart always knew the power of prayers thanks to her.

I always thought I was sure the Catholic religion was my fit and the best way to reach God through a church with. Got baptized, did first communion all through a Catholic Church as my mother did. Senior year of high school I found a modern Christian mega church through one of my closest friends at the time, I fell involve. It was the first time I did not get sidetracked by thoughts during the service, and actually understood the scripture. I felt intrigued the whole time. It was different to what I had been used to my whole life, and it was my very first service in English. A year later my sister introduced me to a church she had been going to for a while. This church was church like I never experienced before. It is relatable, gets you into the church life and true meaning behind it, gets you active and focused and makes sure you truly understand the word of God.

Worship was introduced to me in a bigger better way through this Evangelic mega church. Catholic Churches hadn't introduced me to worshiping the way they do. I loved it and felt like it was my calling from God to keep going back. Two years later I still attend that same church and now serve on the kids group some Sundays. It's okay for it to take some time to find the right church for you. Not every church is for you, just don't give up on finding a way to get closer to God.

Made in the USA
Middletown, DE
22 May 2020